THE OTHER SIDE OF THE RAINBOW
Funny And Quirky Poems That Are Sure To Tickle Your Fancy

By Jason Winchester
Illustrated by Autumn Marble

This poetry book is dedicated to the authors late sister and Mother-in-law,

Jennifer Ellen Winchester (1969-2001)

and

MaryAnne Bartels (1943-2012)

Both women left this world far too early but made a lasting positive impact on everyone they touched.

ABOUT THE AUTHOR

Jason Winchester grew up in the small village of Romeo, Michigan. As a child, he enjoyed playing sports and being creative with art. His mom was an artist that attended Wayne State University in hopes of becoming an Art Teacher. His dad worked for Michigan Bell and helped him build his passion for sports. Being creative was always a part of his home life growing up.

While at Romeo High School, Jason was a member of the varsity baseball and golf teams. After graduation, he attended St. Clair County Community College in Port Huron, Michigan. He received his Associate Degree in Liberal Arts and played baseball. Also, he attended Eastern Michigan University and received a Bachelors Degree in Education.

Jason has been a Physical Education and Health Teacher for Utica Community Schools for the past 15 years. While teaching, he attended Oakland University and received his Masters Degree in Guidance and Counseling. He was a middle school counselor for a few short years. Also, he coached baseball and middle school basketball for several years.

Currently, Jason continues to teach and is married to an Elementary School Teacher. His daughter Chloe is a writing inspiration and gives him ideas everyday. In his free time, Jason enjoys softball, golf and camping. Traveling to Northern Michigan in the summer is his favorite pasttime.

ABOUT THE ILLUSTRATOR

Autumn Marble has always had a love for children's books and art, so illustrating this book was a perfect fit. Autumn has done murals in homes and businesses, designed greeting cards, logos, tattoos and taught art in various settings. Also, she wrote and illustrated a children's book called, "A Cat In A Squirrel's Nest." Autumn received a Bachelor of Science degree in commercial art from Pensacola Christian College and minored in advertising.

Autumn has a family full of "guys." Her husband Tom, has always been supportive of her goals and dreams. Her young boys, West Wyatt and August Christensen, are an important inspiration for her. However, her biggest inspiration and support comes from her faith and lessons learned in life.

Autumn loved illustating, "The Other Side Of The Rainbow", and hopes you feel the words on the page, and be transformed to a place that is on the other side of the rainbow. A warm place where dreams come true and where the sky is not the limit.

WELCOME

Well, Come in.

Pull up a chair and sit for a spell,

Flip through the pages, I have stories to tell.

Places and things far from ordinary,

Some are quite funny while others are scary.

It will take just a minute, a second or two,

Sip on some coffee, a tea that is brewed.

Your mind may drift to a far off place,

Just take off your shoes, it's not a long race.

Well.......Come in!

BASKETBALL JONES

He dribbles,
He passes,
He shoots and dunks,
He blocks,
He steals,
He shuffles and jumps.

He's graceful,
He's fast,
He scores with ease,
Probably because,
We come up to his knees.

Basketball Jones is awesome and great,
Did I mention he stands a mere Seven Foot Eight!

REMOTE CONTROL

What if there was a remote control that could:

    Turn off the sun, turn off the stars,
    Fly to the moon, take us to Mars.

    Do our homework, clean up a mess,
    Tie all our shoes, put on a dress.

    Eat all our broccoli, eat all our peas,
    Cure all our cancers, stop all disease.

    Make us feel happy and never feel sad,
    Turn off our sister, mom or dad,
    I think I'd buy one and be really glad.

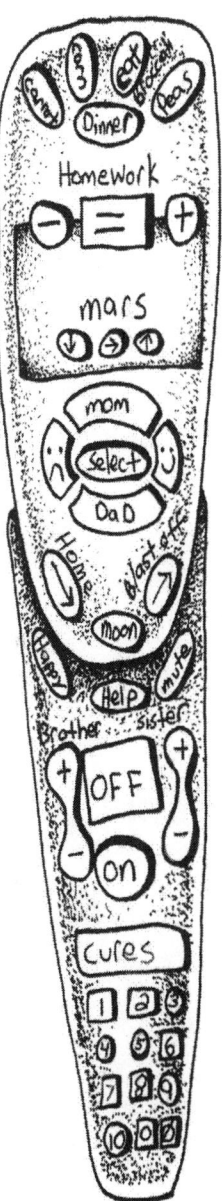

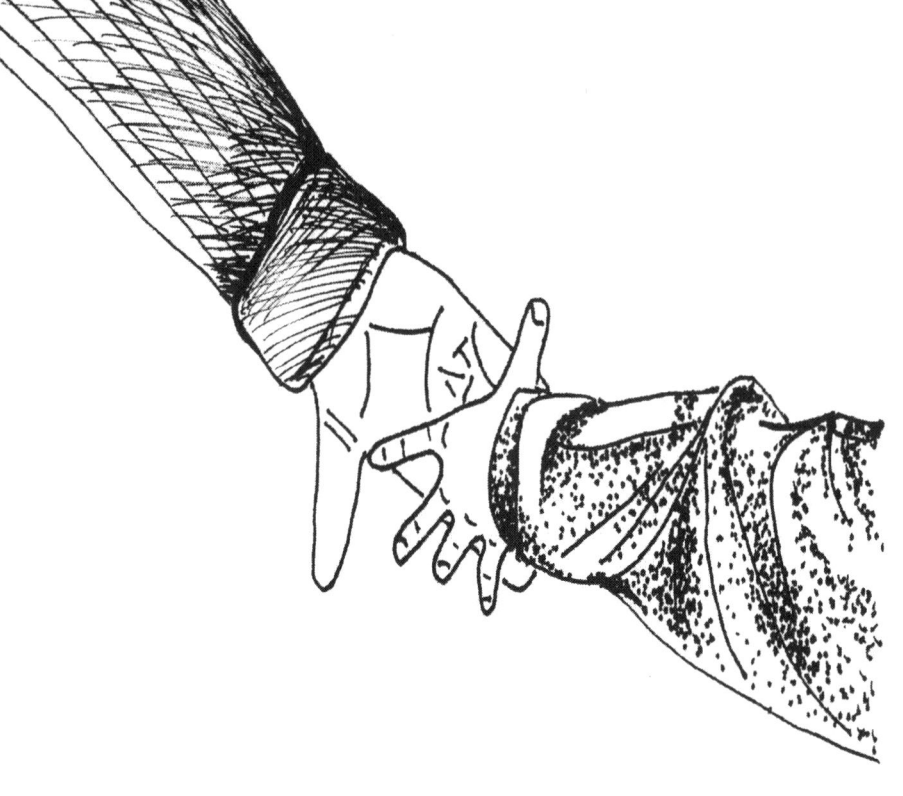

SINGLE PARENT

My mom is a single mother,
My father is a single dad,
I'm glad I have at least the one,
If I had none I'd be really sad.

BOLOGNA

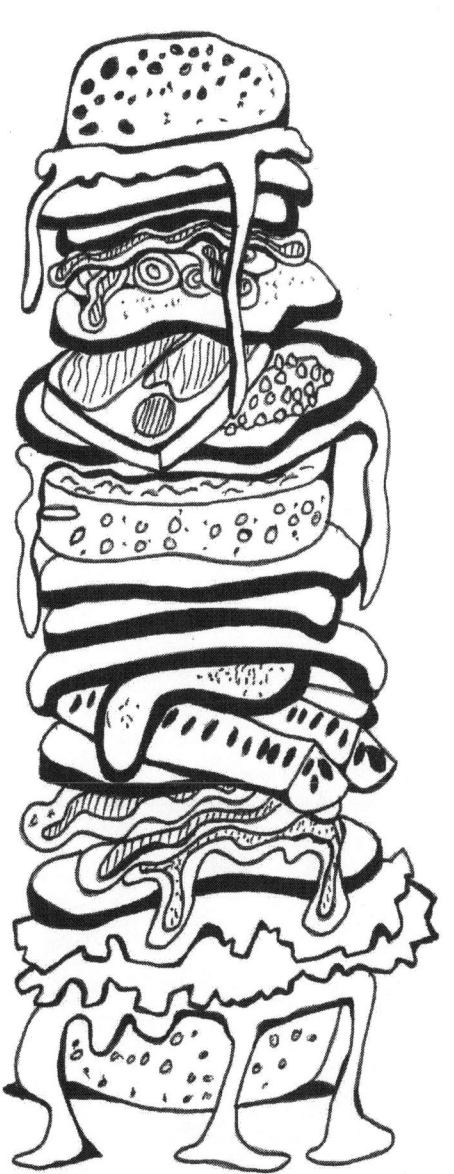

I'd really like to introduce myself,
My name is simply Tony,
And ever since I was a tot,
I only ate bologna.
With ketchup and mustard,
And maybe some bacon,
With relish and salt,
Get the pepper a shakin'.
I ate it with bread,
But sometimes not,
I like it cold,
And love it hot.
Eat it with pickles,
Eat it with steak,
A coke or juice,
Some water a shake.
Bologna with barbaque,
Is the best taste,
I even eat the ends,
Don't leave any waste.
My world would end,
If my bologna ran out,
I guess I would settle,
For some Saurekrat.

COMMON CENTS

If I found a penny,
I'd have good luck.
If I found a hundred,
I'd have a buck.
If I found five cents,
I'd have a nickel.
If I found a few,
I'd buy a pickle.
If I found ten cents,
I'd have a dime.
If I saved a bunch,
I'd buy a poetry rhyme.
If I found twenty-five cents,
I'd have a quarter.
If I had too many,
I'd buy a common cents sorter.
If I found a million pennies,
I'd make a wish,
To have a million more,
Then I'd be rich!

RECESS

Jump Rope, Hopscotch, Hide and Seek,

Kickball, Dodgeball, please don't peek.

I sure would love to play 'em all,

But my Teacher put me on the wall.

I SCREAM

I scream, you scream,
We all scream for ice cream.
Superman and Chocolate Chip,
Butterscotch and Strawberry Dip.
Moosetracks and Rocky Road,
Banana Split and Pie Alamode.
Orange Sherbert in a waffle cone,
Don't wanna share, I'll have my own.
One more scoop I beg you please,
I'll even get down on both my knees.

I think I'll take just one more lick,
Nevermind .... I'm gonna be sick!

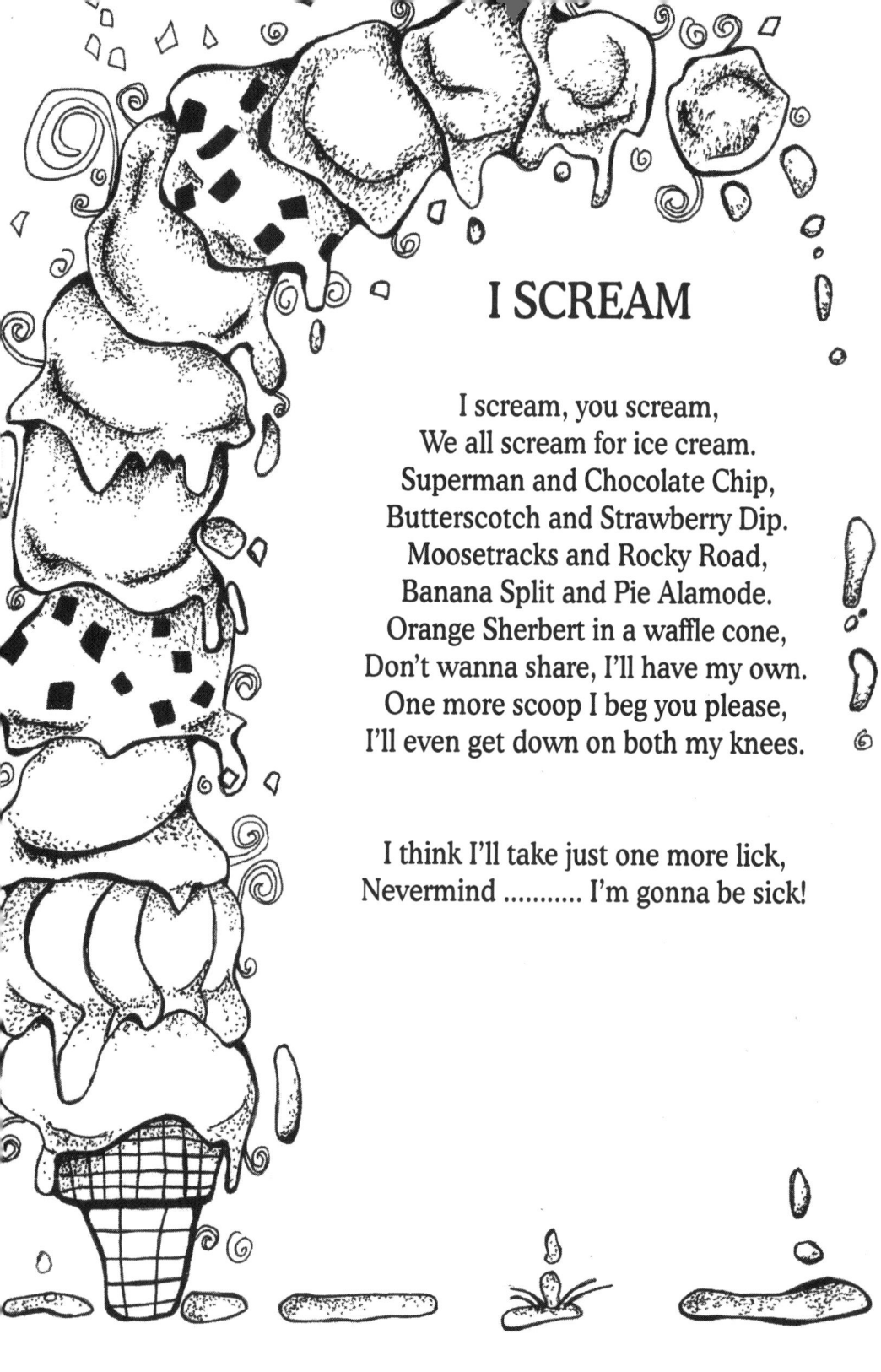

BUCKET LIST

Today I made a bucket list,
Here are just a few things I wished:

Skydive from a plane,
Travel the world on a train.
Climb the Grand Canyon,
Be the best companion.
Swim with a shark,
Don't be afraid of the dark.
Eat a rattlesnake,
While living on a lake.
Feed all the needy,
Don't be so greedy.
Ride on an Elephant,
Pay all my rent.
Fly on a trapeze,
With only my knees,
While I cure a disease,
And not have to say please.
Live in Zimbabwe,
And sleep in everyday.
Have purple hair,
Dance with no care.
Be in a band,
While I live off the land.

Those are just a few things on my list,
I guess the hole in the bottom I musta missed.

WISDOM TEETH

I'm glad I still have my wisdom teeth,
　Set way back and far beneath.

They make me smart and learn a lot,
　I surely hope that they don't rot.

They helped me in my English class,
　With every test that I did pass.

My wisdom teeth I think I need,
　At least to help me when I feed.

But if you take them, make 'em numb,
　I pray it doesn't make me dumb.

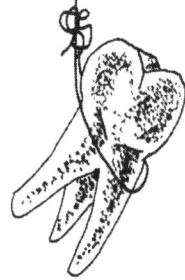

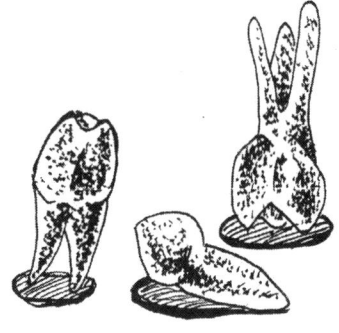

DODGEBALL

Dodging, catching, sliding, slipping,
Throwing, crouching, ducking, dipping.
All great skills while playing the game,
Everyone gets hit so don't feel ashamed.
They hurt real bad everytime they're thrown,
Unless your a kid that plays all alone.

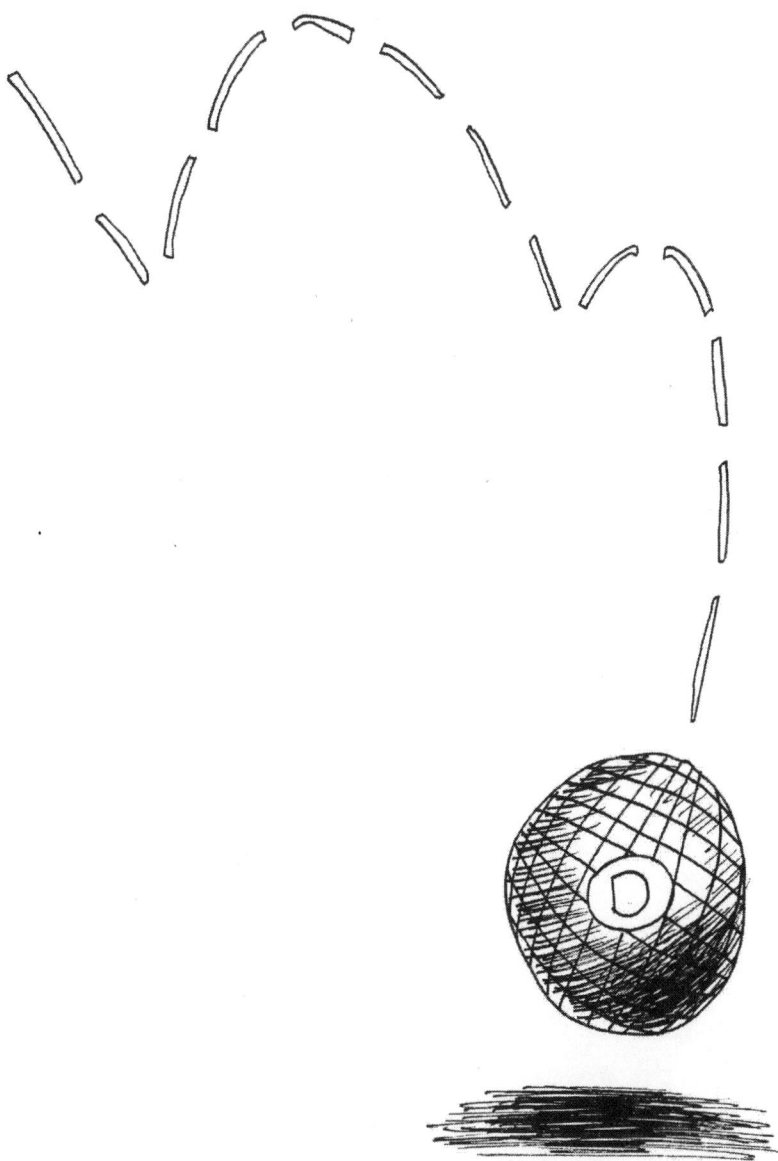

FORK IN THE ROAD

If you come to a stop with a fork in the road,
Please take the one less traveled,
It might have some twists and uneven ground,
And things might become unraveled.

It takes you a place where your creativity blossoms,
And your thoughts and imagination run free,
Far from the suburbs and out past the towns,
Over the hills and beyond all the trees.

Your thoughts of uncertain and confusion will fade,
As you realize you made the right choice,
As long as you remember to follow your dreams,
And listen to only your voice.

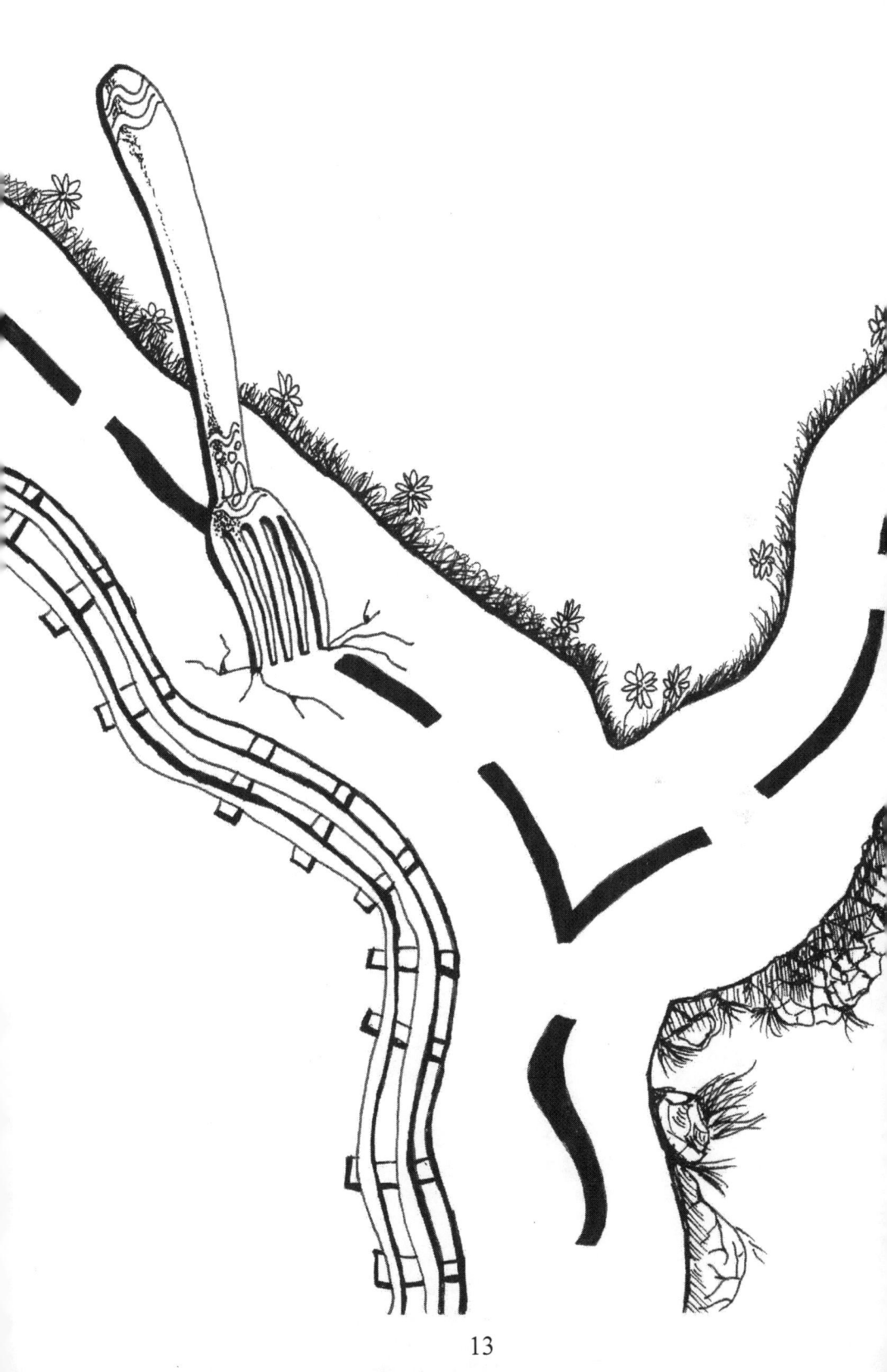

ZOMBIES

Ever met a zombie who didn't want to eat,
Some flesh, bones, hands, and feet.
I met one last week who only ate pies,
No fingers, toes, ears or eyes.
Some apple, blueberry or even cherry,
He wasen't all bloody, he wasn't all scary.
Each night we had our dinner and enjoyed other food,
He seemed pretty normal and a really cool dude.
Until one night he decided to pepper my arm,
I started to panic and had reason for alarm.
I knew right then it was too good to be true,
He grabbed on my arm and started to chew.

MY SWEATER'S BETTER

I really like your sweater,
But mine's a little better.
Yours is too saggy,
And mine's not so baggy.
Yours is too bright,
While mine fits just right.
It's really plain to see,
That you got yours for free.
I take mine everywhere I go,
So people get a sweater show.
I wear it almost everday,
And take good care so it doesn't fray.
It goes with me when I do travel,
So I make sure it does not unravel.

I WONDER...

If bees have knees,
Or fleas have knees.
If pollywogs sit on logs,
And turn in to frogs.
If sheep really sleep,
And chicks really peep.
If cats eat rats,
Or bats are fat.
If cows really moo,
And ghosts really booooo.
If horses are hoarse,
Well, I think, of course.
If dogs really bark,
At trees with bark.
If crows really crow,
and snails really slow.

If penguins don't fly,
Then do Hyenas not cry?

I wonder...

GRAMMA SUE

My Gramma Sue,
Got her 13th tattoo,
We kinda knew,
After a few,
What she would do,
If she had a chance to,
Get another tattoo,
From her old neighbor Drew,
I have to tell you,
It's nothing new,
Like the day Gramma Sue,
Dyed her hair blue.

HEAVEN

Above all the people, above all the crowds,
Atop of the houses, trees and clouds.

There's a place that's bright and full of goodness,
Where we all go to find eternal bliss.

It's not too fancy, it's not too grand,
But there's one thing about it that beats any land.

It's quiet, it's peaceful and everything's free,
You can ask any angel or take it from me.

CAMPING

Camping is funner and camping is neater,
Until you get bit by a really big Skeeter.

Camping is tasty while roasting S'mores,
Until your up all night with someone that snores.

Camping is great when the fire is warm,
Until you step on a hive and the bees start to swarm.

Camping is swell when the sun shines real bright,
Until the sun goes down and lost your flashlight.

Camping is best until you run in to snakes,
And realize that you forgot the tent stakes.

ATHLETE'S FOOT

I have a bad case of athlete's foot,

And it's very plain to see,

So why am I itching it way up high,

I must have athlete's knee.

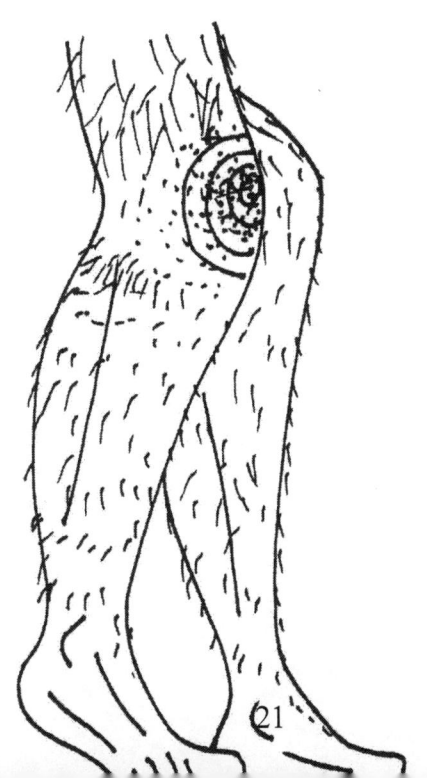

IF LIFE GIVES YOU LEMONS

If life gives you lemons, make lemonade,
If life gives you gators, make Gatorade.

If life gives you snow, make snow cones,
If life gives you kidneys, make kindney stones.

If life gives you grapes, make some wine,
If life gives you sun, make sunshine.

If life gives you peanuts, make peanut butter,
If life gives you mud, make it muddier.

If life gives you lemons and you don't know why,
you might as well make Lemon Meringue Pie.

HOME WORK

I once had homework for eight hours straight,
Get it all done and don't stay up late.
I like my Teacher, I mean she's just fine,
Books stacked to my eyes, don't mean to whine.
Spelling, Reading and even some Math,
Stink so bad, don't have time for a bath.
I get in trouble for not finishing my work,
I guess that makes me one really big jerk.
But I thought about this long and hard,
Just before my last report card..........

What if I didn't have a place to live,
Would that mean there would be no homework to give?

ONE WISH

If I had 1 wish,
It would be for more,
And 3 after that,
Or maybe even 4.
Oh shucks, oh darn,
Forgot about 2,
It's only 1 less,
1 less than a few.
5 is a lot,
And 6 is real grand,
7's too much,
To fit in 1 hand.
8 would be great,
But 9 would be greedy,
If I had a 10th wish,
I'd feed all the needy.

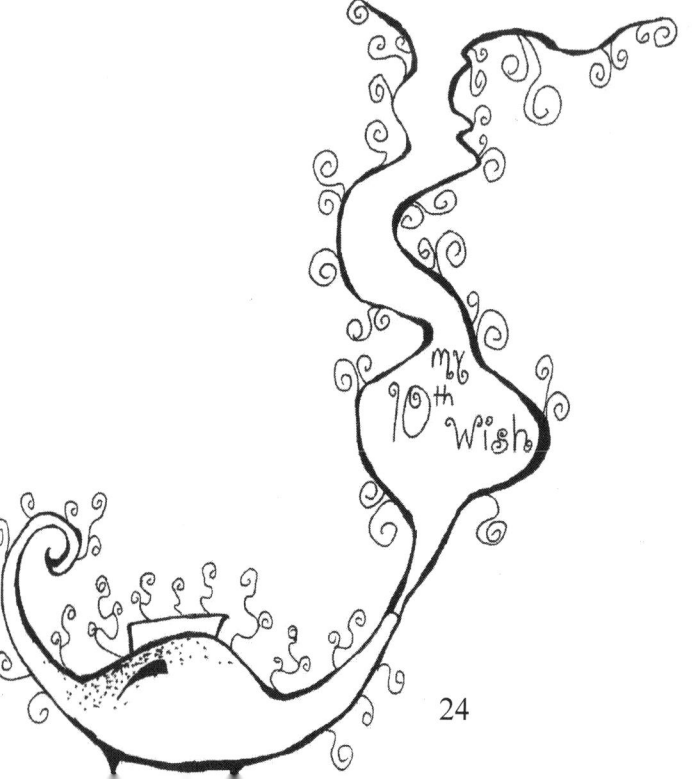

HOMEMADE DISGUISE

Just last year on Halloween,
My mom made me a homemade disguise,
It took me a half a block to realize,
That she forgot to cut out the eyes.

MR. NASH'S MOUSTACHE

I once had a neighbor named old Mr. Nash,
Who had an incredible, unbearable,
extra long moustache.
That whirled and swirled and matched his own hair,
And when he sneezed it flew
through the air.
So long in length, just short of his toes,
In a pinch, that's right he blew his own nose.
It had creatures and critters that built their own nests,
Almost as curly as the hair on his chest.

So thick and wiry, it covered his lip,
He holds it back before taking a sip.
He cleans it with shampoo and never soap,
Us neighborhood kids use it to jump rope.
Sometimes he tucks it in his back jeans,
He's been growing it since the age of eighteen.
One day when brave, as he falls fast asleep,
In his house, at night I will creep.
The moustache, I will grab and take a few hacks,
With some scissors, chainsaw or even an ax.

RECYCLE

Everyone says you should always recycle,
And I think it's probably true,
One thing most of us don't realize,
I bet we're recycled too.

SHOWER

This morning got up and jumped in the shower,

Fell asleep in there for at least an hour,

Got out, dried off and felt real great,

I was wrinkled and pruned and looked 88!

DRAGONSLAYER

I once knew a kid named Timmy McMayer,
Who thought he was a dragonslayer.
He wore a helmet and sword of foam,
To find a dragon til he did roam.
He stumbled upon a dragons lair,
And climbed on in without a care.
He spotted a dragon in his plain sight,
Awoke the dragon for a medieval fight.
The dragon rose up and spit hot fire,
But Timmy stayed strong and did not tire.
The battle went on for six days and a half,
The dragon just smirked and started to laugh.
Reared back his head with one last whisp,
Blew fire so hot that Timmy was crisp.

JOBS

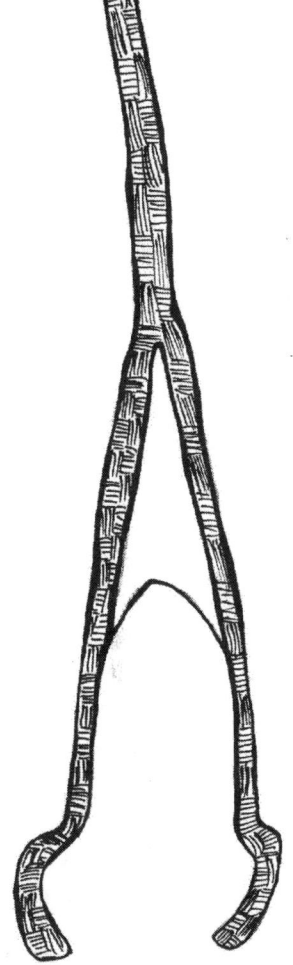

I tried to be a Teacher,
But the kids were too loud,
I tried to be a Celebrity,
But could'nt stand the crowd.

I tried to be a Garbageman,
But didn't like the trash,
I tried to be a Sprinter,
But hated the 100 yard dash.

I tried to be a Gardener,
But wasn't a fan of dirt,
I tried to be a Supermodel,
But didn't look good in a skirt.

I tried to be a Doctor,
But am scared of the blood,
I tried to be a Gravedigger,
But slipped in the mud.

I guess I'm not really cut out for a job,
I guess I'll become a professional slob.

TABLE FOR ONE

I decided to get,
A table for one,
Little did I know,
It would be so much fun.
I ate and ate,
And stuffed my face,
I was the only one,
In the entire place.
I ordered dessert,
With a cherry on top,
I kept on eating,
It was hard to stop.
I looked at the bill,
It was a hundred and three,
The bad news was,
The one paying was me.
The more I ate,
The more my stomach grew,
Next time I go eat,
I'll need a table for two.

FEARS

I know someone that has no fears,
They never cry or have any tears.
Jump out of a plane or a moving train,
Bounce off the pavement and have no pain.
Grab a grenade and pull the pin,
Ride a shark upon it's fin.
Run around naked in the freezing cold,
Grab a bull by the horns and take a strong hold.
This person I knew that had no fears,
He lasted only a few short years.

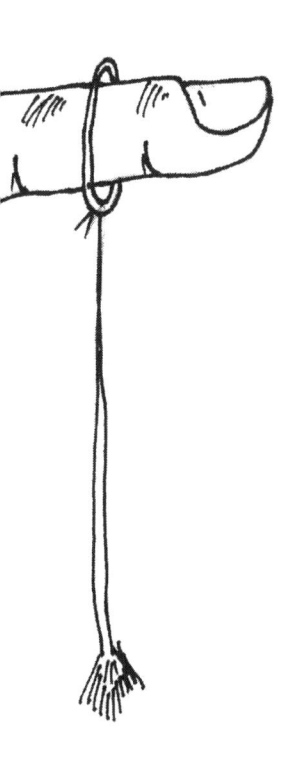

YO-YO

I have this old yo-yo,

That does a few tricks,

There's just one small thing,

That I forgot to fix.

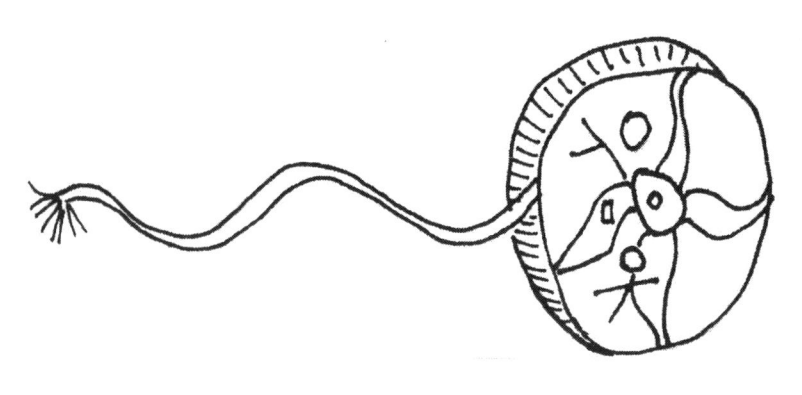

CANCER STINKS

When you're young you would never think,
That when you get older, Cancer would stink.
It's yucky and dark and makes us feel sad,
It's hurtful and painful and makes us real mad.
There are some things I know Cancer can't take,
Here's a small list for goodness sake:
A hope and a dream,
All the memories we've seen.
A walk in the park,
A kiss after dark.
A heart that will mend,
A hug from a friend.
A flower in the wild,
A smile from a child.
A really big thrill,
An undying will.
A wish that comes near it,
A childish spirit,
A thought that can be,
The love of FAMILY.
A dream, a hope, a wish for sure,
That one day mankind will find a CURE.

EAT YER PEAS

My Mama always said, "just eat yer peas,"
But I'd rather eat some Mac and Cheese.

My Mama always said, "You'll go without,"
But I'd rather eat bad Sauerkrat.

My Mama always said," Yer never gonna grow,"
But I'd rather eat some raw cookie dough.

My Mama always said," clean yer plate,"
But I'd rather eat some old fish bait.

My Mama always said,"just eat yer peas,"
So I said," I'd rather go hungry please."

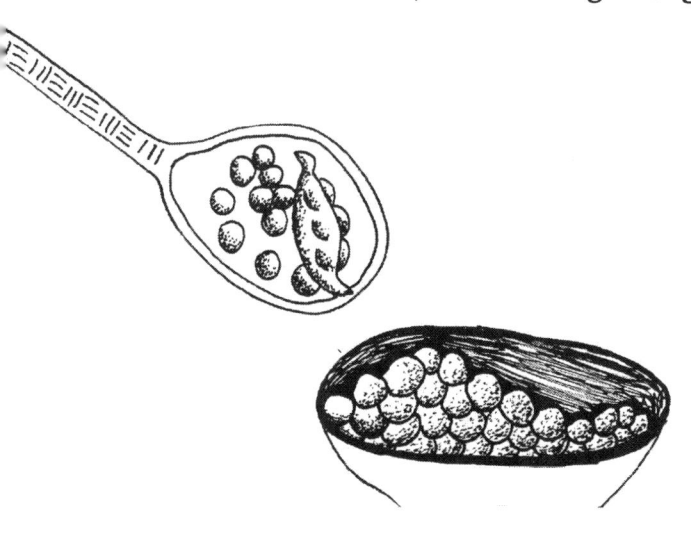

BROTHERS

Can I tell you that I hate my brother,
Talks like my Dad and looks like my Mother.
Yells and screams and throws big fits,
With greasy hair and smelly pits.
Obnoxious, awful and downright rude,
Not a kid you'd wanna see nude.
Always bossy and has to win,
The bad news is, he's also my twin.

SNOW

Early December we decided to go,

Play outside where the wind did blow,

We made snowballs and began to throw,

Joe reared back like he was a Pro,

It flew through the ar and hit 'Ol Moe,

Before we knew it his anger did grow,

From the top of his head to the bottom of his toe,

So Moe picked up a big ball of snow,

Reared back and yelled, "look out below,"

And sorry for Joe well what do you know,

The color of the snow, you guessed it

YELLOW!

BUFFALO WINGS

Buffalo's and birds are not the same,
Birds are fowl and buffalo's are game.
Last I checked they don't have wings,
They have horns, fur and other things.
Eat grass and graze and weigh a ton,
Watching 'em fly would be so much fun.
They'd take up a better part of the sky,
That's why you'd never see 'em fly.
But if you saw one flying by,
Duck and run cause they wouldn't fly high.

SKYSCRAPER

Would you like a job,
Where you dress like a slob,
And work all day next to a guy named Bob.

Take a very long ladder,
To a place full of matter,
To hear the silence and not much chatter.

To dust all the clouds, stars and sun,
Scrape all the pollution until you were done,
Which doesn't sound like too much fun.

I have been told I'm an important guy,
Who has a great job and must qualify,
To save the Earth and clean up the sky.

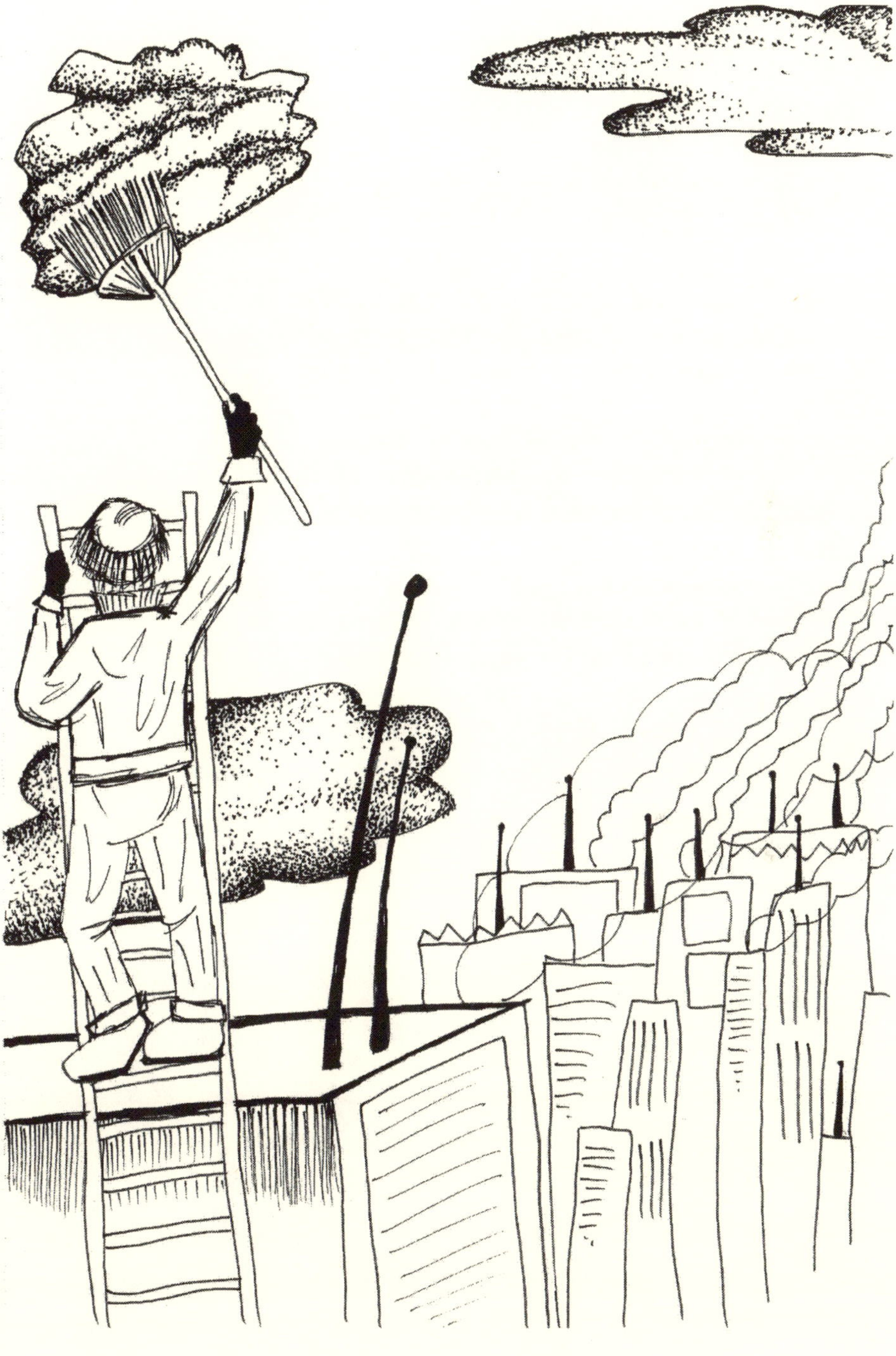

MY PET DINOSAUR

When I was young , I had a pet dinosaur,
He didn't chase people and didn't even roar.
I took him for walks on a leash in the park,
He didn't chase squirrels and surely didn't bark.
He wouldn't fetch a stick or ball,
Beacuse he stood about eight stories tall.
Too big for the house, he slept outside,
He was much too fat and surely too wide.
One day he got sick and came down with the flu,
And turned three shades of yellow, pink and blue.
So we dug and dug the biggest hole yet,
With every bulldozer we could get,
That very sad day we buried my pet,
Because there's no such thing as a dinosaur Vet.

DARK

How come it's always dark at night,

I know why,

Someone turned out the light!

THE OTHER SIDE OF THE RAINBOW

There's a secret place I like to go,
It's on the other side of the rainbow.
It's a very long journey and takes quite a while,
But when you arrive, you are sure to smile.
There's clouds and colors but no pot of gold,
With friendship and family and hands to hold.
It's a spot you can go when you're feeling real blue,
You can sit and just think or find something new.
It doesn't cost money or have any rides,
It's a place to escape when you wanna go hide.
You can sit for a bit or more than a while,
Did I also mention you will leave with a smile.
No matter what hour, no matter what day,
It's a place that we wish we all could stay.
But before I go back to my old boring place,
Of course, with a grin and a smile on my face.
You won't need a map, you'll sure find your way,
If your having a bad minute, hour or day.
So close your eyes real tight and off you go,
To a place that I call, " The Other Side of The Rainbow."

PIZZA

Pizza for breakfast,
Pizza for lunch,
Pizza for dinner,
Pizza for brunch.

Pizza with cheese,
Or pizza without,
Sardines, anchovies,
Or Sauerkrat.

So delicious and yummy,
So grand and great,
I could eat pizza pie,
For 100 days straight.

Round or flat,
And sometimes square,
Don't ask me,
Beacuse I prolly won't share.

All day long,
I could eat pizza pie,
I could eat pizza pie until I die.........
I MIGHT EVEN TRY!

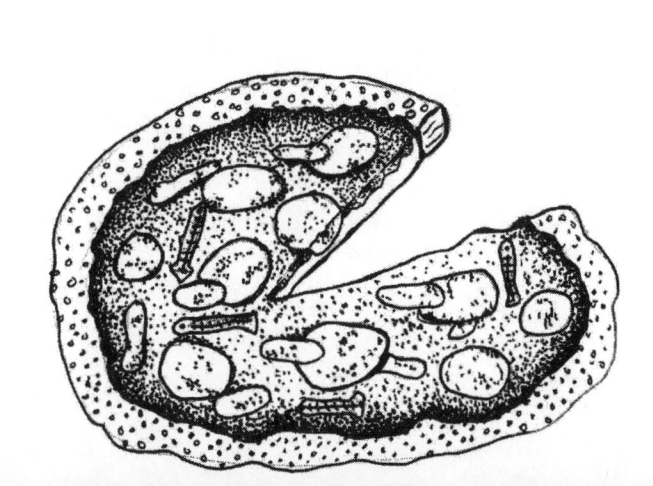

WHY

Why do birds fly and penguins won't,
But flamingo's do and ostrich's don't.

Why do cows heard and buffalo's roam,
And sheep flock but kangaroo's stay home.

Why do hyenas laugh and doves cry,
And bats are blind but owls have great eyes.

Why do zebra's have stripes and rhino's are plain,
And lions have manes and Tarzan has Jane.

So I ask you why do the bees always buzz,
The zookeeper would say, "it's just because."

S'MORES

Chewy,
Sticky,
Ooey,
Icky,
Gooey,
Smushy,
Graham,
Gushy,
Mallow,
Mushy,
Yummy,
Choco,
Tummy,

Tasty,

Pasty,

All over my Facey.

THIN ICE

I hope you really do think twice,
Before you step onto that thin ice.

You might have to creep or even tip toe,
Especially if it's covered with snow.

You must show courage and even some brave,
Cause the outcome could be a watery grave.

So before you take a step too soon,
Make sure it's not the middle of June!

THE WORLD ENDS TOMORROW

What if tomorrow the world would end,
Would you be with your family or your best friend.
Would you take a short trip,
Or skinny dip.
Would you pack a suitcase,
For a far off place.
Would you stop all the crime,
Or spend your last dime.
Would you try a new food,
Or dance in the nude.
Would you smile all day,
Or know what to say.
Would you make your last wish,
Or kiss a real fish.
Would you jump out of a plane,
Or sing in the rain.
Would you fly to Tahiti,
Or make some graffiti.
Would you save all the whales,
Or tell tall tales.
Would you rocket to the moon,
Or act like a baboon.
Would you solve world peace,
Or hunger at least.
Oh by the way.................
The world is ending today!

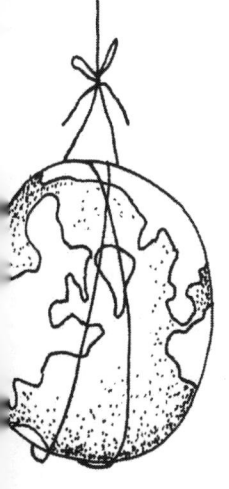

COOTIES

In my Kindergarten class, there's a girl with cooties,
Who always wears sandals and never wears booties.
Her hair stands up and is always a mess,
With stains on her shirt and dirt on her dress.
At recess I watch as she plays all alone,
Just walking around and kicking a stone.
She has no friends, just all enemies,
Maybe beacuse of the dirt on her knees.
One day I decided to give her a smile,
I got one back, but it took quite a while.
The kids all saw and made fun of me,
I picked up some dirt and rubbed it on my knee.
As they were all staring, I gave her a hug,
And out of her shirt popped a tiny little bug.
I told her that day it doesn't matter to me,
If your hair is a mess or stains on your knees.
What matters to me is what's inside,
So she gave me a hug and smiled real wide.
That girl in Kindergarten who had all the cooties,
Is my best friend and her name is Judy.

CHINCHILLA

I have a pet that's real mean and scary,
That's furry and fuzzy and really quite hairy.
His name is Lamar and he's a Chinchilla,
But don't stick your head in cause he's a killa!

FLEA MARKET

I went to a place that only sold fleas,
No ants, no bugs, no flies, no bees.
They all looked the same not one of a kind,
The problem was they were so hard to find.
I searched and searched and finally found,
One tiny flea that fell to the ground.
I picked it up with a finger twitch,
I started to scratch, I started to itch.
Maybe instead, I'll buy a fish or frog,
Now I know what it feels like to be a dog.
I finally decided that I shouldn't get,
One single flea cause their not a good pet.

IMAGINE IF...

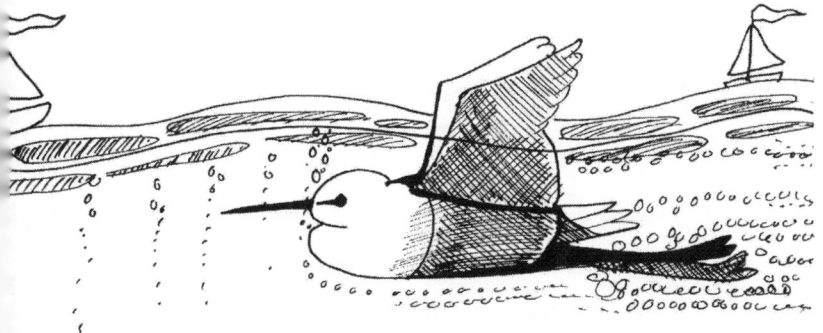

Imagine if the world was actually flat,
And had no trees, imagine that.
Imagine if the sky was purple and not blue,
And birds really swam and fish really flew.
Imagine if Christmas was the 25th of July,
And the 4th of December was hot and dry.
Imagine if dogs meowed and cats barked,
And the moon burned hot and the sun was dark.
Imagine if our enemies could never hate,
And all politicians could never debate.
Imagine if our Teachers were taught by the kids,
And leftovers came without any lids.
Imagine if our moms never met our dads,
I'm not really sure, but I'm certainly glad.

MACK THE LUMBERJACK

Deep in the woods there's a guy named Mack,
Who swings an axe then hears a crack.

On the trees he does attack,
With mighty force and one big hack.

The wood he cuts then lays a stack,
For later use upon his rack.

His tools he carries upon his back,
An axe, a saw and burlap sack.

But for this man, he has a knack,
Of losing fingers and that's a fact.

So if you see him, don't distract,
Cause that's the life of a Lumberjack.

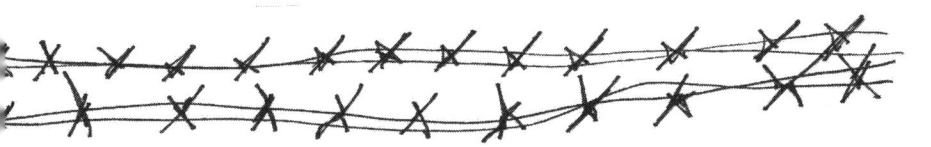

COW TIPPING

In our town, we get really bored,
So outside of town we drive our Ford.
We wait til night when it gets real dark,
Next to the pasture, our Ford we park.
One at a time we tiptoe out,
Without a scream, peep or shout.
Up to the cows we creep real slow,
And wait for someone to yell out, "GO".
With all our might we push and nudge,
But none the less the cows won't budge.
We all line up for a running start,
And hopefully the cows don't fart.
We run full speed and take a leap,
To tip the cow in one big heap.
We grab, takle, prod and pull,
In hopes that we don't grab the Bull.

TREEHUGGER

I love all trees and that's no joke,
An Elm, a Pine, a Birch an Oak.
Trees are great and trees are grand,
I wish trees covered the entire land.
Don't saw 'em off, don't chop 'em down,
Cause you'd see one great big frown.
They keep us alive with oxygen,
My frown would change to one big grin.
A Spruce, a Maple or Hickory,
A tree is what I'd love to be.
I hug all trees, I hug 'em all,
No trees too big, no trees too small.
I love all trees and that's no joke,
Just don't make me hug a Poison Oak!

SMILEY O'REILLY

There once was a girl who always did grin,
From ear to ear and down to her chin.
With red curly hair and Irish descent,
She smiled when she came, she smiled when she went.
Nothing made her cry or even feel sad,
Her mood was always happy and joyfully glad.
Whistled and walked, she would hum a nice tune,
And cheered you right up with a bright red balloon.
To make you feel good she would go out of her way,
And be grateful that she could brighten your day.
I feel thankful that I can call her my friend,
If you need one she has a smile to lend.

TIRE SWING PARTY

It said on the invitiation what to bring,
A present, some rope and your own tire swing.
I climbed up my tree to untie the rope,
Trying not to fall was my only hope.
My friends parties are always so great,
The only rule is, "Don't show up too late."
I arrived kinda late and smelled the cake bakin',
The problem was that all the trees were taken.

NEVER HUG

Never hug a Wolverine,
They're much too nasty and downright mean.
Never hug as Billy Goat,
They'll nibble your scarf and then your coat.
Never hug a Chimpanzee,
They'll squeeze your leg and break your knee.
Never hug a Grizzly Bear,
They'll scratch your back and scalp your hair.
Never hug a Rhinocerous,
They'll sit on you and ooze out puss.
Never hug a Rattlesnake,
They'll squeeze your neck and breath they'll take.
Never hug a Porcupine,
You dont' know............well, nevermind.

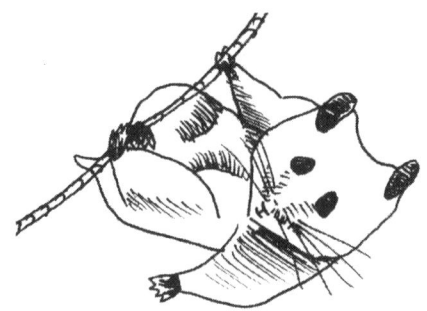

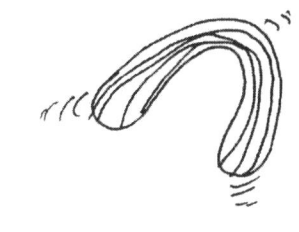

WAR

What if we had war.....

Without guns and tanks,
And bombs and hate,
No pain, no death,
Wouldn't that be great.

You could only fight ......

With slingshots and wet noodles,
And hamsters and poodles,
Or boomerangs and cheese,
and mice and fleas.

I wouldn't mind fighting the war a bit,
No one would protest or have a fit.
They'd be begging for war upon their knees,
With extra large spoons full of macaroni and cheese.

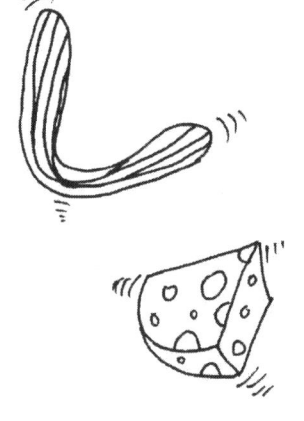

FRECKLES

My freckles cover me from head to toe,
Nobody knows cause none of 'em show.
I've been teased, bullied and called a spot,
Speckled, pimpled and polka dot.
I've tried powder, make-up and even bleach,
On places of my body I could hardly reach.
How I wish they would all fade away,
I scrub and scrub but they continue to stay.
One thing I think that you all should know,
With each passing year, I sure hope they don't grow.

LAMONT FROM VERMONT

There's a guy I know by the name of Lamont,
Who lives way up in the hills of Vermont.
He lives up high in a rickety old shack,
Made by wood that he carried on his back.
He has no heat and no running water,
The food that he eats is the one that he slaughters.
He has long hair and a scraggly beard,
The town folk think he's really quite weird.
He likes to ski, snowboard and hike,
He has a pet dog that rides on his bike.
About this old guy I bet you'd agree,
He's not really like you or like me.
I hope he stays put and decides not to flee,
Pack up all his stuff and move to Tennessee......

He'd have to change his name to
Lee from Tennesse!

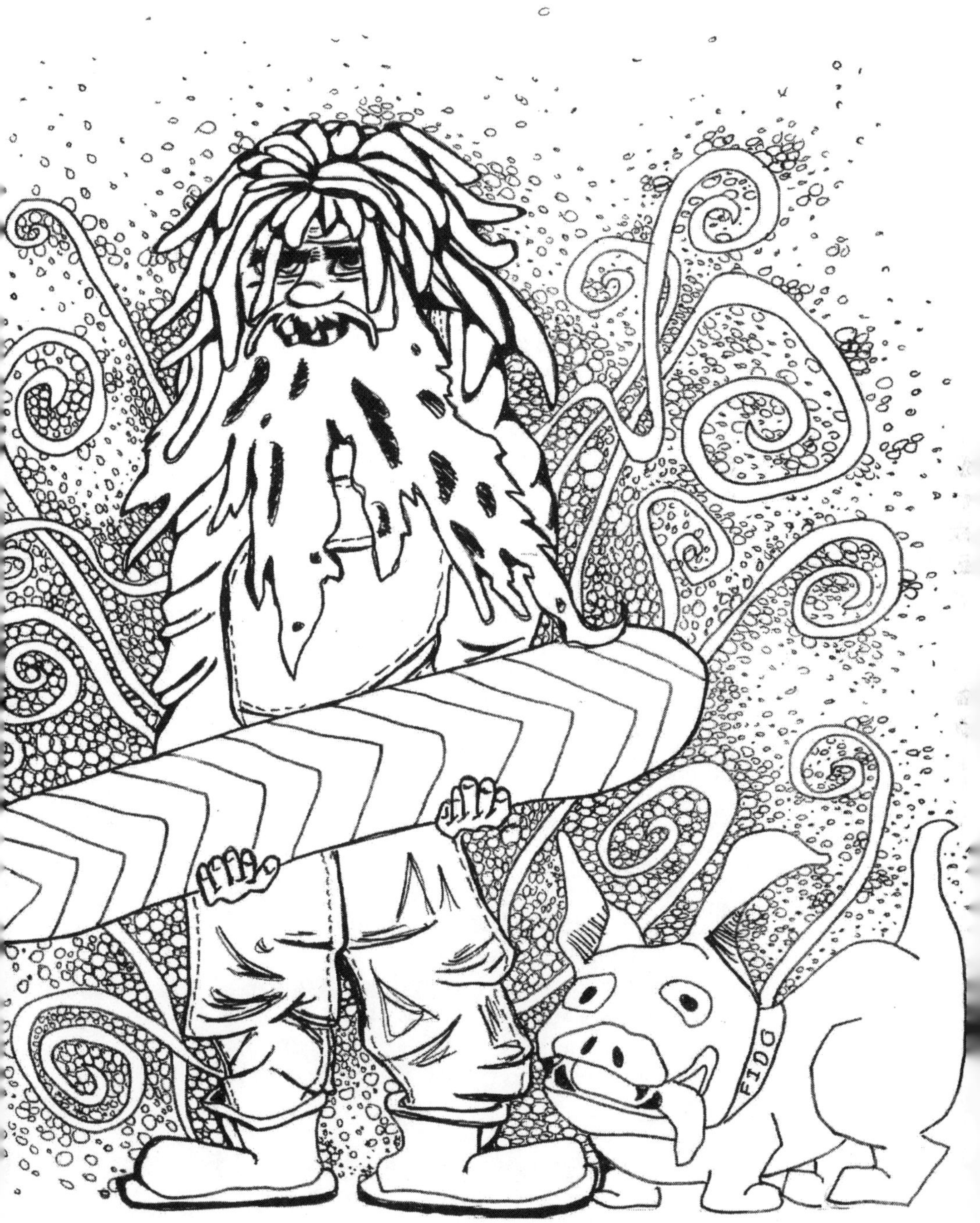
FIDO

IMAGINATION STATION

Beyond the outskirts on the edge of the city,
Stood a factory that was very unpretty.
It had a machine that I'm sad to say,
Took all of the children's imaginations away.
With buttons and blinkers and really big levers,
These machines were ginormous and massive endeavors.
The children became dull and oh so plain,
From Sally to Mary and even to Jane.
No angels, no fairies and no unicorns,
No dragons or cyclops with really big horns.
One night this girl still with her imagination,
Snuck out of her window and down to the station.
She stacked all the boxes and stacked all the crates,
And climbed up the wall on the side of the gates.
She stepped in the shop and to her surprise,
Found the machines too big and enormous in size.
She walked around back overwhelmed at first,
And found a red button tha was labeled, "REVERSE."
The button was pushed as she snuck out of sight,
She just might have saved the children that night.
The next day the machines started to run,
And by our surprise the children had fun.
There were cartwheels, flips and smiling faces,
Laughing and giggling and relay races.
With rainbows, clowns and polka dot wagons,
Leprechans, pixies and fire breathing dragons.
The imaginations were back once and for all,
No dream was too big, no dream was too small.

Reverse

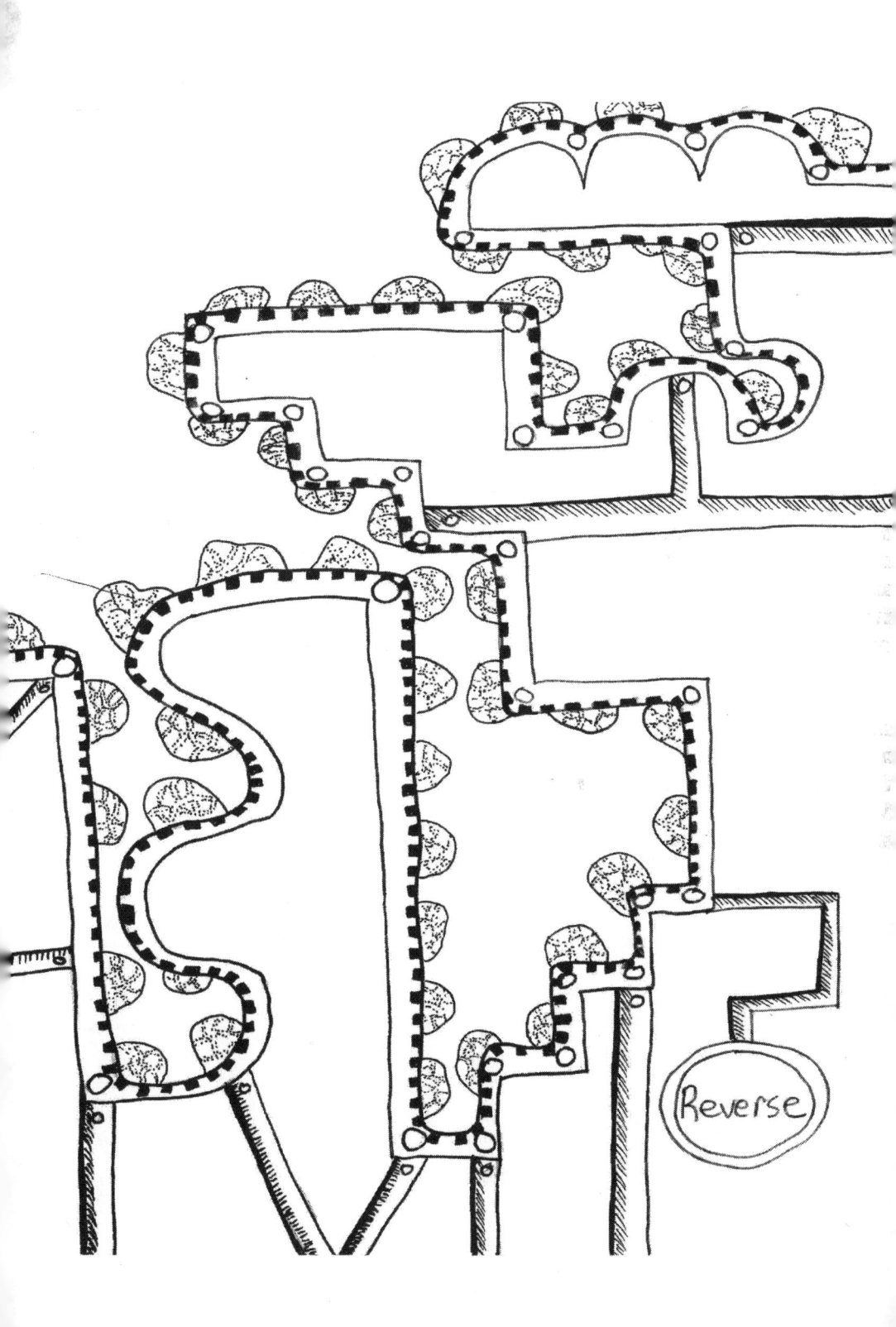

VOODOO DOLL

Yesterday at the store I bought this doll,
And it's very plain to see,
It's full of pricks and little holes,
And looks a lot like me.

The directions said to hurt the doll,
By sticking in some pins,
The doll's supposed to be someone real,
Who has alot of sins.

I shoulda returned the doll,
When I started feeling pain,
Forgot which store and lost the receipt,
Too late, I've gone INSANE.

67

WHINING

No whining,
No crying,
No fighting,
No fussing.
No hitting,
No punching,
No tackling,
No cussing.

If you feel you must have to whine,
Then you must not be a child of mine.

NEIGHBORS

Neighbors are great,
Neighbors are grand,
Neighbors are smart,
Neighbors are bland.
Neighbors are sweet,
Neighbors are sassy,
Neighbors are giving,
Neighbors are classy.

Until one day they notice you're gone,
Creep into your yard and pee on your lawn.

GRANDMOTHER NATURE

Who taught Mother Nature about:

Rain and snow,
Winds that blow,
Lightning to show,
Flowers that grow,
Gardens to hoe,
Birds to crow,
Tornados to slow,
Seeds that sew,
Branches hang low,
Grass to mow,
Snowballs to throw,
I think you might know..........

Grandmother Nature.

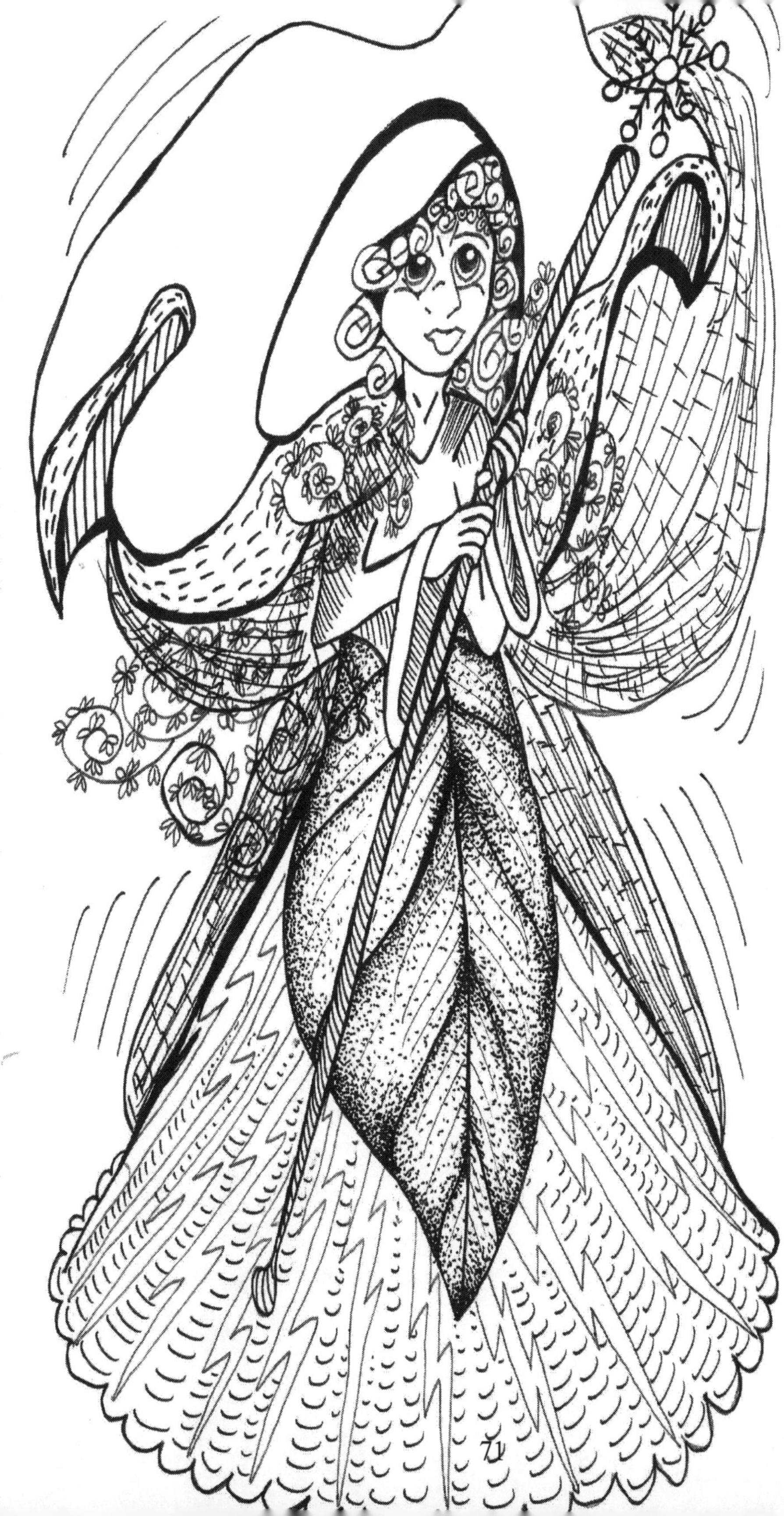

GARAGE SALE

It's not too cheap,
It weighs quite a lot,
It has a few scratches,
It sits in one spot.
My garage is real old,
Fits two and a half cars,
It has several lookers,
But no buyers so far.
For the sucker who buys it,
They may have to prove,
It could take a whole army,
To get it to move.

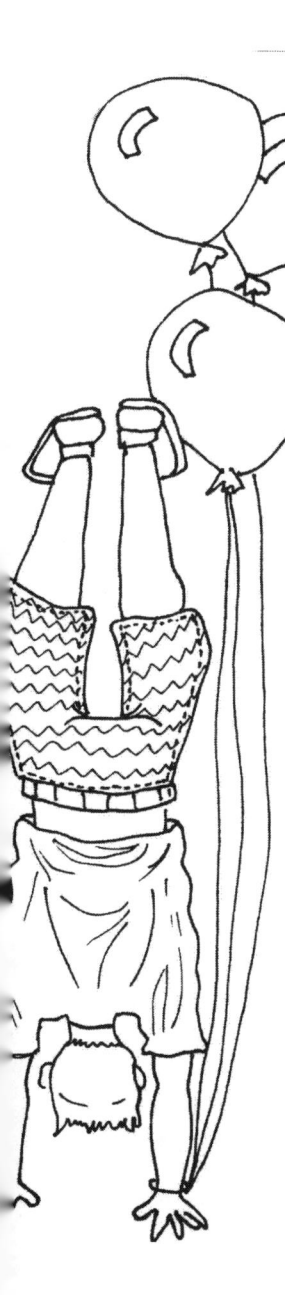

DO I HAVE TO GROW UP

Do I have to grow up and get a real job,
No more grass stained knees, can't dress like a slob.

Do I have to grow up and be an adult,
No more chili dogs with a chocolate malt.

Do I have to grow up and pay all the bills,
No more hide and seek or playground thrills.

Do I have to grow up and dress real nice,
No more buliding forts or chasing mice.

If I have to grow up, I'll wear a big frown,
Do I have to grow up, cause I'd rather grow down.

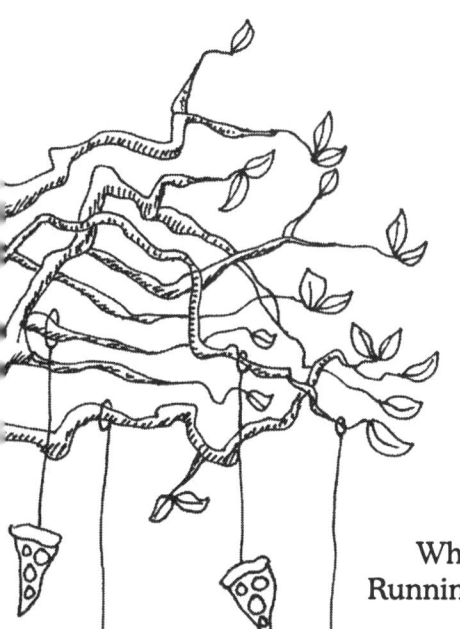

HUNTING

What if humans were hunted by Deer,
Running throught the forest without any fear.

They'd scatter pizza and donuts for bait,
And sit in their stands all day and wait.

They'd put on cologne so we couldn't smell,
Around the campfires, they'd have stories to tell.

They'd sprawl us across the roof of their car,
Cause the drive through the woods isn't too far.

Some short, some fat, some skinny and tall,
Human hunting starts the beginning of Fall.

Never ending stories would be recalled,
We'd look real funny stuffed up on their walls.

YOGA

Stretching a reaching,
Twisting and turning,
My body is aching,
My muscles are burning.

Tranquil and clear,
Peaceful and quiet,
Just one more donut,
Do I have to diet.

This yoga is hard,
That my body can't do,
Is it normal to see,
My ear touching my shoe?

PEACE

Worldly,

Family,

Neighborly,

Eternally,

Brotherly,

Sisterly,

Spiritually,

AND QUIET!

PEACE
FAMILY
WORLDLY
Neighborly
SISTERLY
Brotherly
Eternally
Spiritually
Shhhh zzzzzz's
zzzz's
zzzz's
AND QUIET

Made in the USA
Charleston, SC
02 June 2014